The First & Second Gospels of the Infancy of Jesus Christ

By Thomas and James

ISBN: 978-1-63118-415-4

Christian Apocrypha Series

Other Books in this Series and Related Titles

The Lives of Adam and Eve by Moses
(978-1-63118-414-7)

The Book of the Watchers by Enoch
(978-1-63118-416-1)

Lost Chapters of the Book of Daniel and Related Writings by Daniel
(978-1-63118-417-8)

Symbolism of the Corner Stone, the North East Corner and the Religious &
Masonic Symbolism of Stones by Albert G. Mackey, William Harvey
and William Wynn Westcott
(978-1-63118-412-3)

Ancient Mysteries and Secret Societies by Manly P. Hall
(978-1-63118-410-9)

The Influence of Pythagoras on Freemasonry, the Golden Verses of Pythagoras
and the Life and Philosophy of Pythagoras by Albert G. Mackey and
Manly P. Hall (978-1-63118-320-1)

The Philosophy of Masonry in Five Parts by Roscoe Pound
(978-1-63118-004-0)

Rosicrucian and Masonic Origins by Manly P. Hall
(978-1-63118-000-2)

The Story and Legend of Hiram Abiff by William Harvey, Manly P.
Hall and Albert G. Mackey
(978-1-63118-411-6)

Four Lesser Known Masonic Essays by Frank C. Higgins
(978-1-63118-003-3)

Audio Versions are also Available on Audible and iTunes

Table of Contents

Introduction

The Apocrypha are a loosely knit series of books, written by early vanguards of Christianity (covering the eras of both the old and new testaments), and which comprise somewhere between about a dozen to several hundred titles, depending on whom you ask and how that person defines "Apocrypha." A small selection of these can still be found included in the Catholic bible, while a majority of the books in question, were abandoned by church officials in the early centuries of Christianity. Many of these apocryphal books were originally considered canon by early followers of Christ, in the first four centuries following his birth. It wasn't until the meeting of the Council of Nicaea in 325, that Emperor Constantine and a group of roughly 300 church bishops, gathered together with the goal of defining, standardizing and unifying an otherwise splintering Christianity, that many of these writings ceased to be included in the newly established canon. Enjoy then, this book as an example, of just one of the many books of the Christian Apocrypha, and be sure to check out other titles in this series.

Prologue to the First Gospel

The First Gospel of the Infancy of Jesus Christ, also commonly referred to as The Infancy Gospel of Thomas (*not to be confused with the apocryphal book simply called the Gospel of Thomas*), can safely be dated to the mid second century; although, some scholars date it as early as 80 A.D. In spite of the first written references to the text going back to 185 A.D., the earliest surviving Greek manuscript dates to the 13th century. There also exist some shorter, truncated versions of the gospel in both Syriac and Latin, dating to the 6th century. The text tells stories of the early events in the life of Christ, including miracles; although, also included are stories depicting the childhood Jesus behaving less sacredly than one might expect, which may be exactly the reason why the infancy gospels were never considered canon by the Church. Presented here is a translation of one of the longer Greek versions and one of the longer Latin versions. These translations are from the nineteenth century and were a collaboration between James Donaldson and Alexander Roberts. The pair worked together translating 24 volumes of early Christian texts from Greek and Latin, into English. Numerous manuscripts have turned up over the centuries, with either fragments of the text or shorter versions of the stories therein, some of which have minor differences, and you'll notice some of those differences in these two versions.

PART I

Thomas the Israelite Philosopher's Account of the Infancy of the Lord

(translated from the Greek)

CHAPTER I

I, Thomas, an Israelite, write you this account, that all the brethren from among the heathen may know the miracles of our Lord Jesus Christ in His infancy, which He did after His birth in our country. The beginning of it is as follows:

CHAPTER II

This child Jesus, when five years old, was playing in the ford of a mountain stream; and He collected the flowing waters into pools, and made them clear immediately, and by a word alone He made them obey Him. And having made some soft clay, He fashioned out of it twelve sparrows. And it was the Sabbath when He did these things. And there were also many other children playing with Him. And a certain Jew, seeing what Jesus was doing, playing on the Sabbath, went off immediately, and said to his father Joseph: Behold, thy son is at the stream, and has taken clay, and made of it twelve birds, and has profaned the Sabbath. And Joseph, coming to the place and seeing, cried out to Him, saying: Wherefore doest thou on the Sabbath what it is not lawful to do? And Jesus clapped His hands, and cried out to the sparrows, and said to them: Off you go! And the sparrows flew, and went off crying. And the Jews seeing this were amazed, and went away and reported to their chief men what they had seen Jesus doing.

CHAPTER III

And the son of Annas the scribe was standing there with Joseph; and he took a willow branch, and let out the waters which Jesus bad collected. And Jesus, seeing what was done, was angry, and said to him: O wicked, impious, and foolish! what harm did the pools and the waters do to thee? Behold, even now thou shalt be dried up like a tree, and thou shalt not bring forth either leaves, or root, or fruit. And straightway that boy was quite dried up. And Jesus departed, and went to Joseph's house. But the parents of the boy that had been dried up took him up, bewailing his youth, and brought him to Joseph, and reproached him because, *said they*, thou hast such a child doing such things.

CHAPTER IV

After that He was again passing through the village; and a boy ran up against Him, and struck His shoulder. And Jesus was angry, and said to him: Thou shalt not go back the way thou camest. And immediately he fell down dead. And some who saw what had taken place, said: Whence was this child begotten, that every word of his is certainly accomplished? And the parents of the dead boy went away to Joseph, and blamed him, saying: Since thou hast such a child, it is impossible for thee to live with us in the village; or else teach him to bless, and not to curse: for he is killing our children.

CHAPTER V

And Joseph called the child apart, and admonished Him, saying: Why doest thou such things, and these people suffer, and hate us, and persecute us? And Jesus said: I know that these words of thine are not thine own; nevertheless for thy sake I will be silent; but they shall bear their punishment. And straightway those that accused Him were struck blind. And those who saw it were much afraid and in great perplexity, and said about Him: Every word which he spoke, whether good or bad, was an act, and became a wonder. And when they saw that Jesus had done such a thing, Joseph rose and took hold of His ear, and pulled it hard. And the child was very angry, and said to him: It is enough for thee to seek, and not to find; and most certainly thou hast not done wisely. Knowest thou not that I am thine? Do not trouble me.

CHAPTER VI

And a certain teacher, Zacchaeus by name, was standing in a certain place, and heard Jesus thus speaking to his father; and he wondered exceedingly, that, being a child, he should speak in such a way. And a few days thereafter he came to Joseph, and said to him: Thou hast a sensible child, and he has some mind. Give him to me, then, that he may learn letters; and I shall teach him along with the letters all knowledge, both how to address all the elders, and to honour them as forefathers and fathers, and how to love those of his own age. And He said to him all the letters from the Alpha even to the Omega, clearly and with great exactness. And He looked upon the teacher Zacchaeus, and said to him: Thou who art ignorant of the nature of the Alpha, how canst thou teach others the Beta? Thou hypocrite! first, if thou knowest, teach the A, and then we shall believe thee about the B. Then He began to question the teacher about the first letter, and he was not able to answer Him. And in the hearing of many, the child says to Zacchaeus: Hear, O teacher, the order of the first letter, and notice here how it has lines, and a middle stroke crossing those which thou seest common; (lines) brought together; the highest part supporting them, and again bringing them under one head; with three points *of intersection*; of the same kind; principal and subordinate; of equal length. Thou hast the lines of the A.

CHAPTER VII

And when the teacher Zacchaeus heard the child speaking such and so great allegories of the first letter, he was at a great loss about such a narrative, and about His teaching. And He said to those that were present: Alas! I, wretch that I am, am at a loss, bringing shame upon myself by having dragged this child hither. Take him away, then, I beseech thee, brother Joseph. I cannot endure the sternness of his look; I cannot make out his meaning at all. That child does not belong to this earth; he can tame even fire. Assuredly he was born before the creation of the world. What sort of a belly bore him, what sort of a womb nourished him, I do not know. Alas! my friend, he has carried me away; I cannot get at his meaning: thrice wretched that I am, I have deceived myself. I made a struggle to have a scholar, and I was found to have a teacher. My mind is filled with shame, my friends, because I, an old man, have been conquered by a child. There is nothing for me but despondency and death on account of this boy, for I am not able at this hour to look him in the face; and when everybody says that I have been beaten by a little child, what can I say? And how can I give an account of the lines of the first letter that he spoke about? I know not, O my friends; for I can make neither beginning nor end of him. Therefore, I beseech thee, brother Joseph, take him home. What great thing he is, either god or angel, or what I am to say, I know not.

CHAPTER VIII

And when the Jews were encouraging Zacchaeus, the child laughed aloud, and said: Now let thy learning bring forth fruit, and let the blind in heart see. I am here from above, that I may curse them, and call them to the things that are above, as He that sent me on your account has commanded me. And when the child ceased speaking, immediately all were made whole who had fallen under His curse. And no one after that dared to make Him angry, lest He should curse him, and he should be maimed.

CHAPTER IX

And some days after, Jesus was playing in an upper room of a certain house, and one of the children that were playing with Him fell down from the house, and was killed. And, when the other children saw this, they ran away, and Jesus alone stood still. And the parents of the dead child coming, reproached...and they threatened Him. And Jesus leaped down from the roof, and stood beside the body of the child, and cried with a loud voice, and said: Zeno-for that was his name-stand up, and tell me; did I throw thee down? And he stood up immediately, and said: Certainly not, my lord; thou didst not throw me down, but hast raised me up. And those that saw this were struck with astonishment. And the child's parents glorified God on account of the miracle that had happened, and adored Jesus.

CHAPTER X

A few days after, a young man was splitting wood in the corner, and the axe came down and cut the sole of his foot in two, and he died from loss of blood. And there was a great commotion, and people ran together, and the child Jesus ran there too. And He pressed through the crowd, and laid hold of the young man's wounded foot, and he was cured immediately. And He said to the young man: Rise up now, split the wood, and remember me. And the crowd seeing what had happened, adored the child, saying: Truly the Spirit of God dwells in this child.

CHAPTER XI

And when He was six years old, His mother gave Him a pitcher, and sent Him to draw water, and bring it into the house. But He struck against some one in the crowd, and the pitcher was broken. And Jesus unfolded the cloak which He had on, and filled it with water, and carried it to His mother. And His mother, seeing the miracle that had happened, kissed Him, and kept within herself the mysteries which she had seen Him doing.

CHAPTER XII

And again in seed-time the child went out with His father to sow corn in their land. And while His father was sowing, the child Jesus also sowed one gain of corn. And when He had reaped it, and threshed it, He made a hundred ears; and calling all the poor of the village to the threshing-floor, He gave them the corn, and Joseph took away what was left of the corn. And He was eight years old when He did this miracle.

CHAPTER XIII

And His father was a carpenter, and at that time made ploughs and yokes. And a certain rich man ordered him to make him a couch. And one of what is called the cross pieces being too short, they did not know what to do. The child Jesus said to His father Joseph: Put down the two pieces of wood, and make them even in the middle. And Joseph did as the child said to him. And Jesus stood at the other end, and took hold of the shorter piece of wood, and stretched it, and made it equal to the other. And His father Joseph saw it, and wondered, and embraced the child, and blessed Him, saying: Blessed am I, because God has given me this child.

CHAPTER XIV

And Joseph, seeing that the child was vigorous in mind and body, again resolved that He should not remain ignorant of the letters, and took Him away, and handed Him over to another teacher. And the teacher said to Joseph: I shall first teach him the Greek letters, and then the Hebrew. For the teacher was aware of the trial that had been made of the child, and was afraid of Him. Nevertheless he wrote out the alphabet, and gave Him all his attention for a long time, and He made him no answer. And Jesus said to him: If thou art really a teacher, and art well acquainted with the letters, tell me the power of the Alpha, and I will tell thee the power of the Beta. And the teacher was enraged at this, and struck Him on the head. And the child, being in pain, cursed him; and immediately he swooned away, and fell to the ground on his face. And the child returned to Joseph's house; and Joseph was grieved, and gave orders to His mother, saying: Do not let him go outside of the door, because those that make him angry die.

CHAPTER XV

And after some time, another master again, a genuine friend of Joseph, said to him: Bring the child to my school; perhaps I shall be able to flatter him into learning his letters. And Joseph said: If thou hast the courage, brother, take him with thee. And he took Him with him in fear and great agony; but the child went along pleasantly. And going boldly into the school, He found a book lying on the reading-desk; and taking it, He read not the letters that were in it, but opening His mouth, He spoke by the Holy Spirit, and taught the law to those that were standing round. And a great crowd having come together, stood by and heard Him, and wondered at the ripeness of His teaching, and the readiness of His words, and that He, child as He was, spoke in such a way. And Joseph hearing of it, was afraid, and ran to the school, in doubt lest his master too should be without experience. And the master said to Joseph: Know, brother, that I have taken the child as a scholar, and he is full of much grace and wisdom; but I beseech thee, brother, take him home. And when the child heard this, He laughed at him directly, and said: Since thou hast spoken aright, and witnessed aright, for thy sake he also that was struck down shall be cured. And immediately the other master was cured. And Joseph took the child, and went away home.

CHAPTER XVI

And Joseph sent his son James to tie up wood and bring it home, and the child Jesus also followed him. And when James was gathering the fagots, a viper bit James' hand. And when he was racked *with pain*, and at the point of death, Jesus came near and blew upon the bite; and the pain ceased directly, and the beast burst, and instantly James remained safe and sound.

CHAPTER XVII

And after this the infant of one of Joseph's neighbours fell sick and died, and its mother wept sore. And Jesus heard that there was great lamentation and commotion, and ran in haste, and found the child dead, and touched his breast, and said: I say to thee, child, be not dead, but live, and be with thy mother. And directly it looked up and laughed. And He said to the woman: Take it, and give it milk, and remember me. And seeing this, the crowd that was standing by wondered, and said: Truly this child was either God or an angel of God, for every word of his is a certain fact. And Jesus went out thence, playing with the other children.

CHAPTER XVIII

And some time after there occurred a great commotion while a house was building, and Jesus stood up and went away to the place. And seeing a man lying dead, He took him by the hand, and said: Man, I say to thee, arise, and go on with thy work. And directly he rose up, and adored Him. And seeing this, the crowd wondered, and said: This child is from heaven, for he has saved many souls from death, and he continues to save during all his life.

CHAPTER XIX

And when He was twelve years old His parents went as usual to Jerusalem to the feast of the passover with their fellow-travellers. And after the passover they were coming home again. And while they were coming home, the child Jesus went back to Jerusalem. And His parents thought that He was in the company. And having gone one day's journey, they sought for Him among their relations; and not finding Him, they were in great grief, and turned back to the city seeking for Him. And after the third day they found Him in the temple, sitting in the midst of the teachers, both hearing the law and asking them questions. And they were all attending to Him, and wondering that He, being a child, was shutting the mouths of the elders and teachers of the people, explaining the main points of the law and the parables of the prophets. And His mother Mary coming up, said to Him: Why hast thou done this to us, child? Behold, we have been seeking for thee in great trouble. And Jesus said to them: Why do you seek me? Do you not know that I must be about my Father's business? And the scribes and the Pharisees said: Art thou the mother of this child? And she said: I am. And they said to her: Blessed art thou among women, for God hath blessed the fruit of thy womb; for such glory, and such virtue and wisdom, we have neither seen nor heard ever. And Jesus rose up, and followed His mother, and was subject to His parents. And His mother observed all these things that had happened. And Jesus advanced in wisdom, and stature, and grace. To whom be glory for ever and ever.

Amen.

PART II

Here Beginneth the Treatise of the Boyhood of Jesus According to Thomas

(translated from the Latin)

CHAPTER I

How Mary and Joseph Fled with Him into Egypt

When a commotion took place in consequence of the search made by Herod for our Lord Jesus Christ to kill Him, then an angel said to Joseph: Take Mary and her boy, and flee into Egypt from the face of those who seek to kill Him. And Jesus was two years old when He went into Egypt.

And as He was walking through a field of corn, He stretched forth His hand, and took of the ears, and put them over the fire, and rubbed them, and began to eat.

And when they had come into Egypt, they received hospitality in the house of a certain widow, and they remained in the same place one year.

And Jesus was in His third year. And seeing boys playing, He began to play with them. And He took a dried fish, and put it into a basin, and ordered it to move about. And it began to move about. And He said again to the fish: Throw out thy salt which thou hast, and walk into the water. And it so came to pass. And the neighbors, seeing what had been done, told it to the widow woman in whose house Mary His mother lived. And as soon as she heard it, she thrust them out of her house with great haste.

CHAPTER II

How a Schoolmaster Thrust Him Out of the City

And as Jesus was walking with Mary His mother through the middle of the city market-place, He looked and saw a schoolmaster teaching his scholars. And behold twelve sparrows that were quarrelling fell over the wall into the bosom of that schoolmaster, who was teaching the boys. And seeing this, Jesus was very much amused, and stood still. And when that teacher, saw Him making merry, he said to his scholars with great fury: Go and bring him to me. And when they had carried Him to the master, he seized Him by the ear, and said: What didst thou see, to amuse thee so much? And He said to him: Master, see my hand full of wheat. I showed it to them, and scattered the wheat among them, and they carry it out of the middle of the street where they are in danger; and on this account they fought among themselves to divide the wheat. And Jesus did not pass from the place until it was accomplished. And this being done, the master began to thrust Him out of the city, along with His mother.

CHAPTER III

How Jesus Went Out of Egypt

And, lo, the angel of the Lord met Mary, and said to her: Take up the boy, and return into the land of the Jews, for they who sought His life are dead. And Mary rose up with Jesus; and they proceeded into the city of Nazareth, which is among the possessions of her father. And when Joseph went out of Egypt after the death of Herod, he kept Him in the desert until there should be quietness in Jerusalem on the part of those who were seeking the boy's life. And he gave thanks to God because He had given him understanding, and because he had found favor in the presence of the Lord God. Amen.

CHAPTER IV

What the Lord Jesus Did in the City of Nazareth

It is glorious that Thomas the Israelite and apostle of the Lord gives an account also of the works of Jesus after He came out of Egypt into Nazareth. Understand all of you, my dearest brethren, what the Lord Jesus did when He was in the city of Nazareth; the first chapter of which is as follows:-

And when Jesus was five years old, there fell a great rain upon the earth, and the boy Jesus walked up and down through it. And there was a terrible rain, and He collected it into a fish-pond, and ordered it by His word to become clear. And immediately it became so. Again He took of the clay which was of that fish-pond, and made of it to the number of twelve sparrows. And it was the Sabbath when Jesus did this among the boys of the Jews. And the boys of the Jews went away, and said to Joseph His father: Behold, thy son was playing along with us, and he took clay and made sparrows, which it was not lawful to do on the Sabbath; and he has broken it. And Joseph went away to the boy Jesus, and said to Him: Why hast thou done this, which it was not lawful to do on the Sabbath? And Jesus opened His hands, and ordered the sparrows, saying: Go up into the air, and fly; nobody shall kill you. And they flew, and began to cry out, and praise God Almighty. And the Jews seeing what had happened, wondered, and went away and told the miracles which Jesus had done. But a Pharisee who was with Jesus took an olive branch, and began to let the water out of the fountain which Jesus had made. And when Jesus saw this, He said to him in a rage: Thou impious and ignorant Sodomite, what harm have my works the fountains of water done thee? Behold, thou shalt become like a dry tree, having neither roots, nor leaves, nor fruit. And immediately he dried up, and fell to the ground, and died. And his parents took him away dead, and reproached Joseph, saying: See what thy son has done; teach him to pray, and not to blaspheme.

CHAPTER V

How the Citizens Were Enraged Against Joseph on Account of the Doings of Jesus

And a few days after, as Jesus was walking through the town with Joseph, one of the children ran up and struck Jesus on the arm. And Jesus said to him: So shalt thou not finish thy journey. And immediately he fell to the ground, and died. And those who saw these wonderful things cried out, saying: Whence is that boy? And they said to Joseph: It is not right for such a boy to be among us. And Joseph went and brought Him. And they said to him: Go away from this place; but if thou must live with us, teach him to; pray, and not to blaspheme: hut our children have been killed. Joseph called Jesus, and reproved Him, saying: Why dost thou blaspheme? For these people who live here hate us And Jesus said: I know that these words are not mine, but thine; but I will hold my tongue for thy sake: and let them see to it in their wisdom. And immediately those who were speaking against Jesus became blind. And they walked up and down, and said: All the words which proceed from his mouth are accomplished. And Joseph seeing what Jesus bad done, in a fury seized Him by the ear; and Jesus said to Joseph in anger: It is enough for thee to see me, not to touch me. For thou knowest not who I am; but if thou didst know, thou wouldst not make me angry. And although just now I am with thee, I was made before thee.

CHAPTER VI

How Jesus Was Treated by the Schoolmaster

Therefore a certain man named Zacheus listened to all that Jesus was saying to Joseph, and in great astonishment said to himself: Such a boy speaking in this way I have never seen. And he went up to Joseph, and said: That is an intelligent boy of thine; hand him over to me to learn his letters; and when he has thoroughly learned his letters, I shall teach him honourably, so that he may be no fool. But Joseph answered and said to him: No one can teach him but God alone. You do not believe that that little boy will be of little consequence? And when Jesus heard Joseph speaking in this way, He said to Zacheus: Indeed, master, whatever proceeds from my mouth is true. And before all I was Lord, but you are foreigners. To me has been given the glory of the ages, to you has been given nothing; because I am before the ages. And I know how many years of life thou wilt have, and that thou wilt be carried into exile: and my Father hath appointed this, that thou mayest understand that whatever proceeds from my mouth is true. And the Jews who were standing by, and hearing the words which Jesus spoke, were astonished, and said: We have seen such wonderful things, and heard such words from that boy, as we have never heard, nor are likely to hear from any other human being,-either from the high priests, or the masters, or the Pharisees. Jesus answered and said to them: Why do you wonder? Do you consider it incredible that I have spoken the truth? I know when both you and your fathers were born, and to tell you more, when the world was made: I know also who sent me to you. And when the Jews heard the words which the child had spoken, they wondered, because that they were not able to answer. And, communing with Himself, the child exulted and said: I have told you a proverb; and I know that you are weak and ignorant.

And that schoolmaster said to Joseph: Bring him to me, and I shall teach him letters. And Joseph took hold of the boy Jesus, and led Him to the house of a certain schoolmaster, where other boys were being taught. Now the master in soothing words began to teach Him His letters, and wrote for Him the first line, which is from A to T, and began to stroke Him and teach Him. And that teacher struck the child on the head: and when He had received the blow, the child said to him: I should teach thee, and not thou me; I know the letters which thou wishest to teach me, and I know that you are to me like vessels from which there come forth only sounds, and no wisdom. And, beginning the line, He said the letters from A to T in full, and very fist. And He looked at the master, and said to him: Thou indeed canst not tell us what A and B are; how dost thou wish to teach others? O hypocrite, if thou knowest and will tell me about the A, then will I tell thee about the B. And when that teacher began to tell about the first letter, he was unable to give any answer. And Jesus said to Zacheus: Listen to me, master; understand the first letter. See how it has two lines; advancing in the middle, standing still, giving, scattering, varying, threatening; triple intermingled with double;

at the same time homogeneous, having all common.

And Zacheus, seeing that He so divided the first letter, was stupefied about the first letter, and about such a human being and such learning; and he cried out, and said: Woe's me, for I am quite stupefied; I have brought disgrace upon myself through, that child. And he said to Joseph: I earnestly entreat thee, brother, take him away from me, because I cannot look upon his face, nor hear his mighty words. Because that child can tame fire and bridle the sea: for he was born before the ages. What womb brought him forth, or what mother nursed him, I know not. Oh, my friends, I am driven out of my senses; I have become a wretched laughing-stock. And I said that I had got a scholar; but he has been found to be my master. And my disgrace I cannot get over, because I am an old man; and what to say to him I cannot find. All I have to do is to fall into some grievous illness, and depart from this world; or to leave this town, because all have seen my disgrace. An infant has deceived me. What answer can I give to others, or what words can I say, because he has got the better of me in the first letter? I am struck dumb, O my friends and acquaintances; neither beginning nor end can I find of an answer to him. And now I beseech thee, brother Joseph, take him away from me, and lead him home, because he is a master, or the Lord, or an angel. What to say I do not know. And Jesus turned to the Jews who were with Zacheus, and said to them: Let all not seeing see, and not understanding understand; let the deaf hear, and let those who are dead through me rise again; and those who are exalted, let me call to still higher things, as He who sent me to you hath commanded me. And when Jesus ceased speaking, all who had been affected with any infirmity through His words were made whole. And they did not dare to speak to Him.

CHAPTER VII

How Jesus Raised a Boy to Life

One day, when Jesus was climbing on a certain house, along with the children, He began to play with them. And one of the boys fell down through a back-door, and died immediately: And when the children saw this, they all ran away; but Jesus remained in the house. And when the parents of the boy who had died had come, they spoke against Jesus: Surely it was thou who made him fall down; and they reviled Him. And Jesus, coming down from the house, stood over the dead child, and with a loud voice called out the name of the child: Sinoo, Sinoo, rise and say whether it was I that made thee fall down. And suddenly he rose up, and said: No, my lord. And his parents, seeing such a great miracle done by Jesus, glorified God, and adored Jesus.

CHAPTER VIII

How Jesus Healed a Boy's Foot

And a few days thereafter, a boy in that town was splitting wood, and struck his foot. And a great crowd went to him, and Jesus too went with them. And He touched the foot which had been hurt, and immediately it was made whole. And Jesus said to him: Rise, and split the wood, and remember me. And when the crowd saw the miracles that were done by Him, they adored Jesus, and said: Indeed we most surely believe that Thou art God.

CHAPTER IX

How Jesus Carried Water in a Cloak

And when Jesus was six years old, His mother sent Him to draw water. And when Jesus had come to the fountain, or to the well, there were great crowds there, and they broke His pitcher. And He took the cloak which He had on, and filled it with water, and carried it to His mother Mary. And His mother, seeing the miracles which Jesus had done, kissed Him, and said: O Lord, hear me, and save my son.

CHAPTER X

How Jesus Sowed Wheat

In the time of sowing, Joseph went out to sow wheat, and Jesus followed him. And when Joseph began to sow, Jesus stretched out His hand, and took as much wheat as He could hold in His fist, and scattered it. Joseph therefore came at reaping-time to reap his harvest. Jesus came also, and collected the ears which He had scattered, and they made a hundred pecks of the best grain; and he called the poor, and the widows, and the orphans, and distributed to them the wheat which He had made. Joseph also took a little of the same wheat, for the blessing of Jesus to his house.

CHAPTER XI

How Jesus Made a Short Piece of Wood the Same Length as a Longer One

And Jesus reached the age of eight years, Joseph was a master builder, and used to make ploughs and ox-yokes. And one day a rich man said to Joseph: Master, make me a couch, both useful and beautiful. And Joseph was in distress, because the wood which he had brought for the work was too short. And Jesus said to him: Do not be annoyed. Take hold of this piece of wood by one end, and I by the other; I and let us draw it out. And they did so; and immediately he found it useful for that which he wished. And He said to Joseph: Behold, do the work which thou wishest. And Joseph, seeing what He had done, embraced Him, and said: Blessed am I, because God hath given me such a son.

CHAPTER XII

How Jesus Was Handed Over to Learn His Letters

And Joseph, seeing that He had such favour, and that He was increasing in stature, thought it right to take Him to learn His letters. And he handed Him over to another teacher to be taught. And that teacher said to Joseph: What letters dost thou wish me to teach that boy? Joseph answered and said: First teach him the Gentile letters, and then the Hebrew. For the teacher knew that He was very intelligent, and willingly took Him in hand. And writing for Him the first line, which is A and B, he taught Him for some hours. But Jesus was silent, and made him no answer. Jesus said to the master: If thou art indeed a master, and if thou indeed knowest the letters, tell me the power of the A, and I shall tell thee the power of the B. Then His master was filled with fury, and struck Him on the head. And Jesus was angry, and cursed him; and he suddenly fell down, and died.

And Jesus returned home. And Joseph gave orders to Mary His mother, not to let Him go out of the court of his house.

CHAPTER XIII

How He Was Handed Over to Another Master

Many days after came another teacher, a friend of Joseph, and said to him: Hand him over to me, and I with much sweetness will teach him his letters. And Joseph said to him: If thou art able, take him and teach him. May it be attended with joy. When the teacher had taken Him, he went along in fear and in great firmness, and held Him with exultation. And when He had come to the teacher's house, He found a book lying there, and took it and opened it, and did not read what was written in the book; but opened His mouth, and spoke from the Holy Spirit, and taught the law. And, indeed, all who were standing there listened to Him attentively; and the master sat down beside Him, and listened to Him with pleasure, and entreated Him to teach them more. And a great crowd being gathered together, they heard all the holy teaching which He taught, and the choice words which I came forth from the mouth of Him who, child as He was, spake such things. And Joseph, hearing of this, was afraid, and running ...the master, where Jesus was, said to Joseph: Know, brother, that I have received thy child to teach him or train him; but he is filled with much gravity and wisdom. Lo, now, take him home with joy, my brother; because the gravity which he has, has been given him by the Lord. And Jesus, hearing the master thus speaking, became cheerful, and said: Lo, now, master, thou hast truly said. For thy sake, he who is dead shall rise again. And Joseph took Him home.

CHAPTER XIV

How Jesus Delivered James from the Bite of a Serpent

And Joseph sent James to gather straw, and Jesus followed him. And while James was gathering the straw, a viper bit him; and he fell to the ground, as if dead from the poison. And Jesus seeing this, blew upon his wound; and immediately James was made whole, and the viper died.

CHAPTER XV

How Jesus Raised a Boy to Life

A few days after, a child, His neighbour, died, and his mother mourned for him sore. Jesus, hearing this, went and stood over the boy, and knocked upon his breast, and said: I say to thee, child, do not die, but live. And immediately the child rose up. And Jesus said to the boy's mother: Take thy son, and give him the breast, and remember me. And the crowd, seeing this miracle, said: In truth, this child is from heaven; for already has he freed many souls from death, and he has made whole all that hope in him.

The scribes and Pharisees said to Mary: Art thou the mother of this child? And Mary said: Indeed I am. And they said to her: Blessed art thou among women, since God hath blessed the fruit of thy womb, seeing that He hath given thee such a glorious child, and such a gift of wisdom, as we have never seen nor heard of. Jesus rose up and followed His mother. And Mary kept in her heart all the great miracles that Jesus had done among the people, in healing many that were diseased. And Jesus grew in stature and wisdom; and all who saw Him glorified God the Father Almighty, who is blessed for ever and ever. Amen.

And all these things I Thomas the Israelite have written what I have seen, and have recounted them to the Gentiles and to our brethren, and many other things done by Jesus, who was born in the land of Judah. Behold, the house of Israel has seen all, from the first even to the last; how great signs and wonders Jesus did among them, which were exceedingly good, and invisible to their father, as holy Scripture relates, and the prophets have borne witness to His works in all the peoples of Israel. And He it is who is to judge the world according to the will of immortality, since He is the Son of God throughout all the world. To Him is due all glory and honour for ever, who lives and reigns God through all ages of ages.

Amen.

Prologue to the Second Gospel

The *Second Gospel of the Infancy of Jesus Christ* is also widely known as the *Protevangelium of James*, James, the brother of Jesus, being the traditionally attributed author to these sets of stories. The title of *Protevangelium* refers to chapter 3, verse 15 of the Book of Genesis, and is often considered the first messianic prophecy in the Old Testament. Its inclusion in the title is intended to suggest that this gospel, written by James, predates both the events and the authorship of the four canonical gospels of the Bible, with a date of around 4 A.D. being inferred, based on reference to the death of Herod in the final paragraph. In reality, however, the text likely dates to the mid second century. There are over 140 known Greek manuscripts containing the text of the *Second Gospel of the Infancy Gospel of Jesus Christ*; however, many of these date to the tenth century or later.

Unlike the *First Gospel of the Infancy of Jesus Christ*, the events here deal primarily with the birth of the Virgin Mary herself and her own life during pregnancy and up to the birth of Jesus.

Presented here is a translation of one of the Greek versions. This translation is from the nineteenth century and was a collaboration between James Donaldson and Alexander Roberts. The pair worked together translating 24 volumes of early Christian texts from Greek and Latin, into English.

Part III

The Second Gospel of the Infancy of Jesus Christ:

The Protoevangelium of James:

The Birth of Mary the Holy Mother of God and Very Glorious Mother of Jesus Christ

I

In the records of the twelve tribes of Israel was Joachim, a man rich exceedingly; and he brought his offerings double, saying: There shall be of my superabundance to all the people, and there shall be the offering for my forgiveness to the Lord for a propitiation for me. For the great day of the Lord was at hand, and the sons of Israel were bringing their offerings. And there stood over against him Rubim, saying: It is not meet for thee first to bring thine offerings, because thou hast not made seed in Israel. And Joachim was exceedingly grieved, and went away to the registers of the twelve tribes of the people, saying: I shall see the registers of the twelve tribes of Israel, as to whether I alone have not made seed in Israel. And he searched, and found that all the righteous had raised up seed in Israel. And he called to mind the patriarch Abraham, that in the last day God gave him a son Isaac. And Joachim was exceedingly grieved, and did not come into the presence of his wife; but he retired to the desert, and there pitched his tent, and fasted forty days and forty nights, saying in himself: I will not go down either for food or for drink until the Lord my God shall look upon me, and prayer shall be my food and drink.

II

And his wife Anna mourned in two mournings, and lamented in two lamentations, saying: I shall bewail my widowhood; I shall bewail my childlessness. And the great day of the Lord was at hand; and Judith her maid-servant said: How long dost thou humiliate thy soul? Behold, the great day of the Lord is at hand, and it is unlawful for thee to mourn. But take this head-band, which the woman that made it gave to me; for it is not proper that I should wear it, because I am a maid-servant, and it has a royal appearance. And Anna said: Depart from me; for I have not done such things, and the Lord has brought me very low. I fear that some wicked person has given it to thee, and thou hast come to make me a sharer in thy sin. And Judith said: Why should I curse thee, seeing that the Lord hath shut thy womb, so as not to give thee fruit in Israel? And Anna was grieved exceedingly, and put off her garments of mourning, and cleaned her head, and put on her wedding garments, and about the ninth hour went down to the garden to walk. And she saw a laurel, and sat under it, and prayed to the Lord, saying: O God of our fathers, bless me and hear my prayer, as Thou didst bless the womb of Sarah, and didst give her a son Isaac.

III

And gazing towards the heaven, she saw a sparrow's nest in the laurel, and made a lamentation in herself, saying: Alas! who begot me? and what womb produced me? because I have become a curse in the presence of the sons of Israel, and I have been reproached, and they have driven me in derision out of the temple of the Lord. Alas! to what have I been likened? I am not like the fowls of the heaven, because even the fowls of the heaven are productive before Thee, O Lord. Alas! to what have I been likened? I am not like the beasts of the earth, because even the beasts of the earth are productive before Thee, O Lord. Alas! to what have I been likened? I am not like these waters, because even these waters are productive before Thee, O Lord. Alas! to what have I been likened? I am not like this earth, because even the earth bringeth forth its fruits in season, and blesseth Thee, O Lord.

IV

And, behold, an angel of the Lord stood by, saying: Anna, Anna, the Lord hath heard thy prayer, and thou shalt conceive, and shall bring forth; and thy seed shall be spoken of in all the world. And Anna said: As the Lord my God liveth, if I beget either male or female, I will bring it as a gift to the Lord my God; and it shall minister to Him in holy things all the days of its life. And, behold, two angels came, saying to her: Behold, Joachim thy husband is coming with his flocks. For an angel of the Lord went down to him, saying: Joachim, Joachim, the Lord God hath heard thy prayer Go down hence; for, behold, thy wife Anna shall conceive. And Joachim went down and called his shepherds, saying: Bring me hither ten she-lambs without spot or blemish, and they shall be for the Lord my God; and bring me twelve tender calves, and they shall be for the priests and the elders; and a hundred goats for all the people. And, behold, Joachim came with his flocks; and Anna stood by the gate, and saw Joachim coming, and she ran and hung upon his neck, saying: Now I know that the Lord God hath blessed me exceedingly; for, behold the widow no longer a widow, and I the childless shall conceive. And Joachim rested the first day in his house.

V

And on the following day he brought his offerings, saying in himself: If the Lord God has been rendered gracious to me, the plate on the priest's forehead will make it manifest to me. And Joachim brought his offerings, and observed attentively the priest's plate when he went up to the altar of the Lord, and he saw no sin in himself. And Joachim said: Now I know that the Lord has been gracious unto me, and has remitted all my sins. And he went down from the temple of the Lord justified, and departed to his own house. And her months were fulfilled, and in the ninth month Anna brought forth. And she said to the midwife: What have I brought forth? and she said: A girl. And said Anna: My soul has been magnified this day. And she laid her down. And the days having been fulfilled, Anna was purified, and gave the breast to the child, and called her name Mary.

VI

And the child grew strong day by day; and when she was six months old, her mother set her on the ground to try whether she could stand, and she walked seven steps and came into her bosom; and she snatched her up, saying: As the Lord my God liveth, thou shall not walk on this earth until I bring thee into the temple of the Lord. And she made a sanctuary in her bed-chamber, and allowed nothing common or unclean to pass through her. And she called the undefiled daughters of the Hebrews, and they led her astray. And when she was a year old, Joachim made a great feast, and invited the priests, and the scribes, and the elders, and all the people of Israel. And Joachim brought the child to the priests; and they blessed her, saying: O God of our fathers, bless this child, and give her an everlasting name to be named in all generations. And all the people said: So be it, so be it, amen. And he brought her to the chief priests; and they blessed her, saying: O God most high, look upon this child, and bless her with the utmost blessing, which shall be for ever. And her mother snatched her up, and took her into the sanctuary of her bed-chamber, and gave her the breast. And Anna made a song to the Lord God, saying: I will sing a song to the Lord my God, for He hath looked upon me, and hath taken away the reproach of mine enemies; and the Lord hath given the fruit of His righteousness, singular in its kind, and richly endowed before Him. Who will tell the sons of Rubim that Anna gives suck? Hear, hear, ye twelve tribes of Israel, that Anna gives suck. And she laid her to rest in the bed-chamber of her sanctuary, and went out and ministered unto them. And when the supper was ended, they went down rejoicing, and glorifying the God of Israel.

VII

And her months were added to the child. And the child was two years old, and Joachim said: Let us take her up to the temple of the Lord, that we may pay the vow that we have vowed, lest perchance the Lord send to us, and our offering be not received. And Anna said: Let us wait for the third year, in order that the child may not seek for father or mother. And Joachim said: So let us wait. And the child was three years old, and Joachim said: Invite the daughters of the Hebrews that are undefiled, and let them take each a lamp, and let them stand with the lamps burning, that the child may not turn back, and her heart be captivated from the temple of the Lord. And they did so until they went up into the temple of the Lord. And the priest received her, and kissed her, and blessed her, saying: The Lord has magnified thy name in all generations. In thee, on the last of the days, the Lord will manifest His redemption to the sons of Israel. And he set her down upon the third step of the altar, and the Lord God sent grace upon her; and she danced with her feet, and all the house of Israel loved her.

VIII

And her parents went down marveling, and praising the Lord God, because the child had not turned back. And Mary was in the temple of the Lord as if she were a dove that dwelt there, and she received food from the hand of an angel. And when she was twelve years old there was held a council of the priests, saying: Behold, Mary has reached the age of twelve years in the temple of the Lord. What then shall we do with her, test perchance she defile the sanctuary of the Lord? And they said to the high priest: Thou standest by the altar of the Lord; go in, and pray concerning her; and whatever the Lord shall manifest unto thee, that also will we do. And the high priest went in, taking the robe with the twelve bells into the holy of holies; and he prayed concerning her. And behold an angel of the Lord stood by him, saying unto him: Zacharias, Zacharias, go out and assemble the widowers of the people, and let them bring each his rod; and to whomsoever the Lord shall show a sign, his wife shall she be. And the heralds went out through all the circuit of Judaea, and the trumpet of the Lord sounded, and all ran.

IX

And Joseph, throwing away his axe, went out to meet them; and when they had assembled, they went away to the high priest, taking with them their rods. And he, taking the rods of all of them, entered into the temple, and prayed; and having ended his prayer, he took the rods and came out, and gave them to them: but there was no sign in them, and Joseph took his rod last; and, behold, a dove came out of the rod, and flew upon Joseph's head. And the priest said to Joseph, Thou hast been chosen by lot to take into thy keeping the virgin of the Lord. But Joseph refused, saying: I have children, and I am an old man, and she is a young girl. I am afraid lest I become a laughing-stock to the sons of Israel. And the priest said to Joseph: Fear the Lord thy God, and remember what the Lord did to Dathan, and Abiram, and Korah; how the earth opened, and they were swallowed up on account of their contradiction. And now fear, O Joseph, lest the same things happen in thy house. And Joseph was afraid, and took her into his keeping. And Joseph said to Mary: Behold, I have received thee from the temple of the Lord; and now I leave thee in my house, and go away to build my buildings, and I shall come to thee. The Lord will protect thee.

X

And there was a council of the priests, saying: Let us make a veil for the temple of the Lord. And the priest said: Call to me the undefiled virgins of the family of David. And the officers went away, and sought, and found seven virgins. And the priest remembered the child Mary, that she was of the family of David, and undefiled before God. And the officers went away and brought her. And they brought them into the temple of the Lord. And the priest said: Choose for me by lot who shall spin the gold, and the white, and the fine linen, and the silk, and the blue, and the scarlet, and the true purple. And the true purple and the scarlet fell to the lot of Mary, and she took them, and went away to her house. And at that time Zacharias was dumb, and Samuel was in his place until the time that Zacharias spake. And Mary took the scarlet, and span it.

XI

And she took the pitcher, and went out to fill it with water. And, behold, a voice saying: Hail, thou who hast received grace; the Lord is with thee; blessed art thou among women! And she looked round, on the right hand and on the left, to see whence this voice came. And she went away, trembling, to her house, and put down the pitcher; and taking the purple, she sat down on her seat, and drew it out. And, behold, an angel of the Lord stood before her, saying: Fear not, Mary; for thou hast found grace before the Lord of all, and thou shalt conceive, according to His word. And she hearing, reasoned with herself, saying: Shall I conceive by the Lord, the living God? and shall I bring forth as every woman brings forth? And the angel of the Lord said: Not so, Mary; for the power of the Lord shall overshadow thee: wherefore also that holy thing which shall be born of thee shall be called the Son of the Most High. And thou shalt call His name Jesus, for He shall save His people from their sins. And Mary said: Behold, the servant of the Lord before His face: let it be unto me according to thy word.

XII

And she made the purple and the scarlet, and took them to the priest. And the priest blessed her, and said: Mary, the Lord God hath magnified thy name, and thou shall be blessed in all the generations of the earth. And Mary, with great joy, went away to Elizabeth her kinswoman, and knocked at the door. And when Elizabeth heard her, she threw away the scarlet, and ran to the door, and opened it; and seeing Mary, she blessed her, and said: Whence is this to me, that the mother of my Lord should come to me? for, behold, that which is in me leaped and blessed thee. But Mary had forgotten the mysteries of which the archangel Gabriel had spoken, and gazed up into heaven, and said: Who am I, O Lord, that all the generations of the earth should bless me? And she remained three months with Elizabeth; and day by day she grew bigger. And Mary being afraid, went away to her own house, and hid herself from the sons of Israel. And she was sixteen years old when these mysteries happened.

XIII

And she was in her sixth month; and, behold, Joseph came back from his building, and, entering into his house, he discovered that she was big with child. And he smote his face, and threw himself on the ground upon the sackcloth, and wept bitterly, saying: With what face shall I look upon the Lord my God? and what prayer shall I make about this maiden? because I received her a virgin out of the temple of the Lord, and I have not watched over her. Who is it that has hunted me down? Who has done this evil thing in my house, and defiled the virgin? Has not the history of Adam been repeated in me? For just as Adam was in the hour of his singing praise, and the serpent came, and found Eve alone, and completely deceived her, so it has happened to me also. And Joseph stood up from the sackcloth, and called Mary, and said to her: O thou who hast been cared for by God, why hast thou done this and forgotten the Lord thy God? Why hast thou brought low thy soul, thou that wast brought up in the holy of holies, and that didst receive food from the hand of an angel? And she wept bitterly, saying: I am innocent, and have known no man. And Joseph said to her: Whence then is that which is in thy womb? And she said: As the Lord my God liveth, I do not know whence it is to me.

XIV

And Joseph was greatly afraid, and retired from her, and considered what he should do in regard to her. And Joseph said: If I conceal her sin, I find myself fighting against the law of the Lord; and if I expose her to the sons of Israel, I am afraid lest that which is in her be from an angel, and I shall be found giving up innocent blood to the doom of death. What then shall I do with her? I will put her away from me secretly. And night came upon him; and, behold, an angel of the Lord appears to him in a dream, saying: Be not afraid for this maiden, for that which is in her is of the Holy Spirit; and she will bring forth a Son, and thou shall call His name Jesus, for He will save His people from their sins. And Joseph arose from sleep, and glorified the God of Israel, who had given him this grace; and he kept her.

XV

And Annas the scribe came to him, and said: Why hast thou not appeared in our assembly? And Joseph said to him: Because I was weary from my journey, and rested the first day. And he turned, and saw that Mary was with child. And he ran away to the priest? and said to him: Joseph, whom thou didst vouch for, has committed a grievous crime. And the priest said: How so? And he said: He has defiled the virgin whom he received out of the temple of the Lord, and has married her by stealth, and has not revealed it to the sons of Israel. And the priest answering, said: Has Joseph done this? Then said Annas the scribe: Send officers, and thou wilt find the virgin with child. And the officers went away, and found it as he had said; and they brought her along with Joseph to the tribunal. And the priest said: Mary, why hast thou done this? and why hast thou brought thy soul low, and forgotten the Lord thy God? Thou that wast reared in the holy of holies, and that didst receive food from the hand of an angel, and didst hear the hymns, and didst dance before Him, why hast thou done this? And she wept bitterly, saying: As the Lord my God liveth, I am pure before Him, and know not a man. And the priest said to Joseph: Why hast thou done this? And Joseph said: As the Lord liveth, I am pure concerning her. Then said the priest: Bear not false witness, but speak the truth. Thou hast married her by stealth, and hast not revealed it to the sons of Israel, and hast not bowed thy head under the strong hand, that thy seed might be blessed. And Joseph was silent.

XVI

And the priest said: Give up the virgin whom thou didst receive out of the temple of the Lord. And Joseph burst into tears. And the priest said: I will give you to drink of the water of the ordeal of the Lord, and He shall make manifest your sins in your eyes. And the priest took the water, and gave Joseph to drink and sent him away to the hill-country; and he returned unhurt. And he gave to Mary also to drink, and sent her away to the hill-country; and she returned unhurt. And all the people wondered that sin did not appear in them. And the priest said: If the Lord God has not made manifest your sins, neither do I judge you. And he sent them away. And Joseph took Mary, and went away to his own house, rejoicing and glorifying the God of Israel.

XVII

And there was an order from the Emperor Augustus, that all in Bethlehem of Judaea should be enrolled. And Joseph said: I shall enroll my sons, but what shall I do with this maiden? How shall I enroll her? As my wife? I am ashamed. As my daughter then? But all the sons of Israel know that she is not my daughter. The day of the Lord shall itself bring it to pass as the Lord will. And he saddled the ass, and set her upon it; and his son led it, and Joseph followed. And when they had come within three miles, Joseph turned and saw her sorrowful; and he said to himself: Likely that which is in her distresses her. And again Joseph turned and saw her laughing. And he said to her: Mary, how is it that I see in thy face at one time laughter, at another sorrow? And Mary said to Joseph: Because I see two peoples with my eyes; the one weeping and lamenting, and the other rejoicing and exulting. And they came into the middle of the road, and Mary said to him: Take me down from off the ass, for that which is in me presses to come forth. And he took her down from off the ass, and said to her: Whither shall I lead thee, and cover thy disgrace? for the place is desert.

XVIII

And he found a cave there, and led her into it; and leaving his two sons beside her, he went out to seek a midwife in the district of Bethlehem. And I Joseph was walking, and was not walking; and I looked up into the sky, and saw the sky astonished; and I looked up to the pole of the heavens, and saw it standing, and the birds of the air keeping still. And I looked down upon the earth, and saw a trough lying, and work-people reclining: and their hands were in the trough. And those that were eating did not eat, and those that were rising did not carry it up, and those that were conveying anything to their mouths did not convey it; but the faces of all were looking upwards. And I saw the sheep walking, and the sheep stood still; and the shepherd raised his hand to strike them, and his hand remained up. And I looked upon the current of the river, and I saw the mouths of the kids resting on the water and not drinking, and all things in a moment were driven from their course.

XIX

And I saw a woman coming down from the hill-country, and she said to me: O man, whither art thou going? And I said: I am seeking a Hebrew midwife. And she answered and said unto me: Art thou of Israel? And I said to her: Yes. And she said: And who is it that is bringing forth in the cave? And I said: A woman betrothed to me. And she said to me: Is she not thy wife? And I said to her: It is Mary that was reared in the temple of the Lord, and I obtained her by lot as my wife. And yet she is not my wife, but has conceived of the Holy Spirit. And the midwife said to him: Is this true? And Joseph said to her: Come and see. And the midwife went away with him. And they stood in the place of the cave, and behold a luminous cloud overshadowed the cave. And the midwife said: My soul has been magnified this day, because mine eyes have seen strange things -- because salvation has been brought forth to Israel. And immediately the cloud disappeared out of the cave, and a great light shone in the cave, so that the eyes could not bear it. And in a little that light gradually decreased, until the infant appeared, and went and took the breast from His mother Mary. And the midwife cried out, and said: This is a great day to me, because I have seen this strange sight. And the midwife went forth out of the cave, and Salome met her. And she said to her: Salome, Salome, I have a strange sight to relate to thee: a virgin has brought forth -- a thing which her nature admits not of. Then said Salome: As the Lord my God liveth, unless I thrust in my finger, and search the parts, I will not believe that a virgin has brought forth.

XX

And the midwife went in, and said to Mary: Show thyself; for no small controversy has arisen about thee. And Salome put in her finger, and cried out, and said: Woe is me for mine iniquity and mine unbelief, because I have tempted the living God; and, behold, my hand is dropping off as if burned with fire. And she bent her knees before the Lord, saying: O God of my fathers, remember that I am the seed of Abraham, and Isaac, and Jacob; do not make a show of me to the sons of Israel, but restore me to the poor; for Thou knowest, O Lord, that in Thy name I have performed my services, and that I have received my reward at Thy hand. And, behold, an angel of the Lord stood by her, saying to her: Salome, Salome, the Lord hath heard thee. Put thy hand to the infant, and carry it, and thou wilt have safety and joy. And Salome went and carried it, saying: I will worship Him, because a great King has been born to Israel. And, behold, Salome was immediately cured, and she went forth out of the cave justified. And behold a voice saying: Salome, Salome, tell not the strange things thou hast seen, until the child has come into Jerusalem.

XXI

And, behold, Joseph was ready to go into Judaea. And there was a great commotion in Bethlehem of Judaea, for Magi came, saying: Where is he that is born king of the Jews? for we have seen his star in the east, and have come to worship him. And when Herod heard, he was much disturbed, and sent officers to the Magi. And he sent for the priests, and examined them, saying: How is it written about the Christ? where is He to be born? And they said: In Bethlehem of Judaea, for so it is written. And he sent them away. And he examined the Magi, saying to them: What sign have you seen in reference to the king that has been born? And the Magi said: We have seen a star of great size shining among these stars, and obscuring their light, so that the stars did not appear; and we thus knew that a king has been born to Israel, and we have come to worship him. And Herod said: Go and seek him; and if you find him, let me know, in order that I also may go and worship him. And the Magi went out. And, behold, the star which they had seen in the east went before them until they came to the cave, and it stood over the top of the cave. And the Magi saw the infant with His mother Mary; and they brought forth from their bag gold, and frankincense, and myrrh. And having been warned by the angel not to go into Judaea, they went into their own country by another road.

XXII

And when Herod knew that he had been mocked by the Magi, in a rage he sent murderers, saying to them: Slay the children from two years old and under. And Mary, having heard that the children were being killed, was afraid, and took the infant and swaddled Him, and put Him into an ox-stall. And Elizabeth, having heard that they were searching for John, took him and went up into the hill-country, and kept looking where to conceal him. And there was no place of concealment. And Elizabeth, groaning with a loud voice, says: O mountain of God, receive mother and child. And immediately the mountain was cleft, and received her. And a light shone about them, for an angel of the Lord was with them, watching over them.

XXIII

And Herod searched for John, and sent officers to Zacharias, saying: Where hast thou hid thy son? And he, answering, said to them: I am the servant of God in holy things, and I sit constantly in the temple of the Lord: I do not know where my son is. And the officers went away, and reported all these things to Herod. And Herod was enraged, and said: His son is destined to be king over Israel. And he sent to him again, saying: Tell the truth; where is thy son? for thou knowest that thy life is in my hand. And Zacharias said: I am God's martyr, if thou sheddest my blood; for the Lord will receive my spirit, because thou sheddest innocent blood at the vestibule of the temple of the Lord. And Zacharias was murdered about daybreak. And the sons of Israel did not know that he had been murdered.

XXIV

But at the hour of the salutation the priests went away, and Zacharias did not come forth to meet them with a blessing, according to his custom. And the priests stood waiting for Zacharias to salute him at the prayer, and to glorify the Most High. And he still delaying, they were all afraid. But one of them ventured to go in, and he saw clotted blood beside the altar; and he heard a voice saying: Zacharias has been murdered, and his blood shall not be wiped up until his avenger come. And hearing this saying, he was afraid, and went out and told it to the priests. And they ventured in, and saw what had happened; and the fretwork of the temple made a wailing noise, and they rent their clothes from the top even to the bottom. And they found not his body, but they found his blood turned into stone. And they were afraid, and went out and reported to the people that Zacharias had been murdered. And all the tribes of the people heard, and mourned, and lamented for him three days and three nights. And after the three days, the priests consulted as to whom they should put in his place; and the lot fell upon Simeon. For it was he who had been warned by the Holy Spirit that he should not see death until he should see the Christ in the flesh.

And I James that wrote this history in Jerusalem, a commotion having arisen when Herod died, withdrew myself to the wilderness until the commotion in Jerusalem ceased, glorifying the Lord God, who had given me the gift and the wisdom to write this history. And grace shall be with them that fear our Lord Jesus Christ, to whom be glory to ages of ages. Amen.

Made in the USA
Middletown, DE
28 March 2021